Message
in a Bottle

Story by Julie Ellis

Illustrations by Suzie Byrne

PM Plus Chapter Books
Ruby Level 27

U.S. Edition © 2013 Houghton Mifflin Harcourt Publishing Company
125 High Street
Boston, MA 02110
www.hmhco.com

Text © 2003 Cengage Learning Australia Pty Limited
Illustrations © 2003 Cengage Learning Australia Pty Limited
Originally published in Australia by Cengage Learning Australia

13   1957   20
4500791898

Text: Julie Ellis
Illustrations: Suzie Byrne
Reprint: Siew Han Ong
Printed in China by 1010 Printing International Ltd

Message in a Bottle
ISBN 978 0 75 786887 0

Contents

Chapter 1

A Find

It was freezing at the beach, but Emily didn't care. The beach had always been Patch's favorite place.

"He'd be chasing seagulls if he were here now," she thought. "Why did he have to die?"

Angrily, Emily snatched up a stick of driftwood, and threw it into the sand dunes. There was a loud *ting* as it hit something, which startled her. She went to investigate.

The stick was lying beside a partly buried bottle, which Emily carefully uncovered. The bottle was dark green, and it sparkled in the sunlight. It looked old-fashioned and mysterious.

Emily lifted the bottle out of the sand, and held it up to the sun. To her surprise, she saw that there was something inside!

"Cool!" she said to herself. "A message in a bottle!"

She tried to pull the cork from the top of the bottle, but it was jammed tight. "Maybe Mom will be able to open it," she said. She slipped the bottle into her pocket and headed home.

When she got home, Emily showed Mom the bottle. "What a beautiful bottle!" said Mom. "It's the perfect bottle for a message from a stranger!"

"Why would anyone put a message in a bottle?" asked Emily. "What if no one ever found it?"

"Long ago, sailors used to put messages in bottles and throw them into the sea," replied Mom. "They were sending their thoughts to their families. It didn't matter if no one ever found the messages – just writing them helped the sailors to feel closer to the people they loved."

Mom pulled hard on the cork, and it came out of the bottle with a loud pop. "Let's have a look at this message!" she said. She pulled a rolled-up piece of paper out of the bottle, and handed it to Emily.

Emily read the message aloud:

Hi to whoever finds this message!

My name is Fiona, and I am 10 years old. I live on a farm. I go to school in Murgon.

 I have a twin brother called Stu, and a dog named Maxi. Maxi is my best friend. I like to take her for walks along the beach. I also like running and playing computer games.

Bye,
Fiona

"What a great message!" said Emily excitedly. "I wish Fiona had put her address on it. I'd love to write back to her, to tell her that I found the bottle."

"She did say that she goes to school in Murgon," said Mom. "Maybe if you took the message to school, Mrs. Brooker would help you to find Fiona's school."

"Great idea, Mom!" said Emily. "I'll take it tomorrow!"

Chapter 2

Seeking Fiona

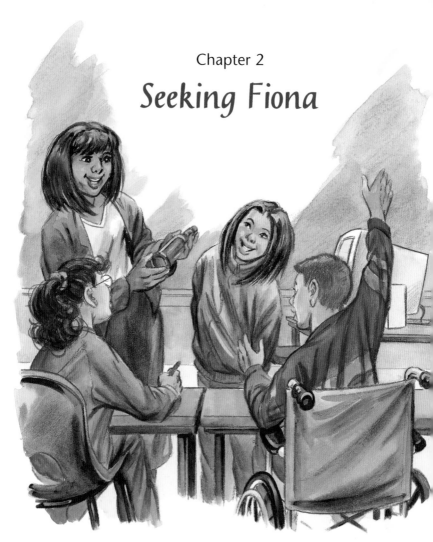

Mrs. Brooker was intrigued by Emily's find. She suggested that the whole class join in the search for Fiona's school. "We could use the Internet to help us," she said. "Now, how could we start?"

"We could search for *Murgon*," suggested Ryan, one of the boys in Emily's class.

"Good idea, Ryan," said Mrs. Brooker.

The computer found two listings for *Murgon*. One was a place called Murgon Farm; the other was called Murgon Apple Grove. But there was no mention of a school in Murgon.

"That's no use," said Ryan in a frustrated voice. "We still don't know how to contact Fiona."

"Fiona lives on a farm," said Emily. "I could e-mail Murgon Farm, to see if that's where she lives. I could also try Murgon Apple Grove, to see if they can help."

She typed out her e-mail.

| Subject: | Seeking Fiona | Date: | March 18 |

Hello,

I am looking for a girl named Fiona, who lives on a farm in Murgon. Do you know her? She is 10. She has a dog named Maxi, and a brother named Stu. I found a message from her in a bottle, and I want to write to her.

Thank you,
Emily

Then she sent it to the addresses that they had found on the Internet. "I hope this works!" she thought.

Later that day, Emily checked the e-mails. Would there be a response from Murgon Farm?

There wasn't. "Oh well," she thought. "Maybe tomorrow."

Chapter 3

Message in a Bottle

As Emily walked home from school, she thought about Fiona's note. Fiona seemed like the perfect penpal for Emily. She liked running and playing computer games. More importantly, she knew what it was like to have a dog for a best friend. Emily was sure that Fiona would understand how much she missed Patch.

But what if she never found Fiona?

She remembered what Mom had said about the sailors who sent messages in bottles. Just writing the letters had helped them to feel closer to their families.

Then she had an idea. "Why don't I just send Fiona a message in a bottle?" she thought. "I could tell her about Patch. Even if she never found the bottle, it would help me to feel closer to her – and to Patch."

Emily quickly ran home. She sat down at her desk, and began to write:

Dear Fiona,

I found your message in a bottle on the beach near my house ...

She told Fiona all about how sad she'd been when Patch died. As she wrote, happy memories of Patch came flooding back – their walks along the beach, how cute he'd been as a puppy, the games they had played together.

When she'd finished, she rolled up the letter, poked it into the bottle, and sealed it with the cork. Then she headed back to the beach.

When she got there, she ran to the water's edge and threw the bottle into the water. A wave broke over the top of it, and it was gone. She sighed. She still hoped that she'd find the real Fiona, but sending her own message in a bottle was the next best thing.

As she walked home, she imagined her bottle drifting in the waves, and wondered where it would end up.

Chapter 4

Success!

When Emily's class checked their e-mails the next day, there were two messages for Emily. With Mrs. Brooker and the rest of the class looking on, Emily opened the first e-mail. It was from Murgon Farm.

Subject:	Seeking Fiona	Date:	March 19

Dear Emily,

I'm sorry, but there's no one here named Fiona.

I hope you find her.

Good luck!
Mrs. Greene

Emily was disappointed.

"Try the other one," Ryan suggested impatiently.

Emily opened the e-mail from Murgon Apple Grove.

Subject:	Seeking Fiona	Date:	March 19

Dear Emily,

Hi! I'm Fiona. I have a twin brother named Stu, and a dog named Maxi.

I can't believe you found my message! I threw it into the waves months ago. Afterward, I realized that I hadn't included my address. I didn't think I'd ever get a reply!

Where do you live? Is it near the beach? (I love the beach!) What school do you go to? What's it like? I go to Riverside School. How old are you? I'm 11 now.

Do you have any pets? You already know about Maxi – she's the best dog in the world!

Write back soon. We can be penpals!

Bye, from your "message in a bottle" friend, Fiona

Emily couldn't believe it. Her e-mail had worked! She quickly wrote back.

Subject:	Hooray!		Date:	March 19

Hi Fiona!

I'm glad I found you! Your message in the bottle was so cool!

I live in Wellington, near the beach. (I love the beach too!) I go to Wellington Elementary School, and I'm 11 years old.

I used to have a dog named Patch. But he got hit by a car a few months ago, and died. I really miss him. I used to take him for walks on the beach – just like you and Maxi. Mom told me that I could get a new dog, but I don't think I want to. It wouldn't be the same.

Do you like living on a farm?
Emily

"I'm really pleased that you found Fiona," said Mrs. Brooker.

"Me too," said Emily. "We're going to be penpals!"

"It would be cool to have an e-mail penpal!" said Ryan. "Maybe we could all write to Fiona."

"It might be a bit difficult for her to write back to all of you," said Mrs. Brooker with a laugh. "But it *would* be nice if you had your own penpals ..."

She thought for a minute, then said, "What if I got in touch with Fiona's teacher? Now that we know the name of her school, it should be easy to find the phone number. Maybe we could arrange penpals in Murgon for each of you. It would be a great way for you to learn about life in the country."

"That *would* be great!" said Emily. The rest of the class agreed.

Chapter 5

Penpals

A few days later, Emily received another e-mail from Fiona.

Subject:	Poor Patch	Date:	March 24

Hi Emily,

Isn't it great that we can e-mail each other at school? When Mr. Murphy told us that your teacher wanted our two classes to be penpals, I was really excited – and so was the rest of my class!

Stu was matched up with someone named Ryan. What's he like?

Mr. Murphy says it's funny that a message in a bottle could still bring people together. He said something about messages in bottles being a really old way for people to communicate, and e-mails being really new. (But I'm glad e-mails are faster than bottles!)

Living on a farm is great. We have sheep and apple trees. We also have some chickens, and a horse named Barney. Stu and I have to do chores, to help Mom and Dad. I like feeding the chickens most.

I was really sad when I read about Patch. You must have been so upset. I'd hate it if anything happened to Maxi.

Fiona

Subject:	How embarrassing!	Date:	March 25

Dear Fiona,

Guess what? The local newspaper heard that I found a message in a bottle, and they came to interview me! They even took a photo!

I'll mail you a copy of the paper when it comes out next week.

Maxi sounds like a great dog. Can you send a picture of her?

Emily

| Subject: | The photos | Date: | April 5 |

Hi Emily,

The newspaper arrived this morning. It's great! Now I know what you look like.

I've attached a scanned photo of Maxi and me. It's one of my favorites!

Fiona

Chapter 6

Great News!

As the weeks passed, Emily, Fiona, and their classmates e-mailed each other regularly. They all agreed that it was the best school project they'd ever done!

Before long, Emily and Fiona were the best of friends. They told each other *everything*. Fiona told Emily all about life on a farm, and Emily told Fiona about life in the city.

Emily told Fiona how much she missed Patch. It was nice to have someone who understood. She even told Fiona about the message in a bottle that *she* had sent to Fiona! "You'll probably never find it," she wrote, "but I thought it would be fun to try! I included my e-mail address, in case someone else finds it!"

★ ★ ★

One day, Emily got an exciting e-mail from Fiona.

| Subject: | Guess what? | Date: | April 22 |

Hi Emily,

Mom and Dad said that I could invite you to visit us during the summer! You can sleep in my room, if you don't mind sleeping on a foldaway bed!

Please say you'll come! We can swim in the river, and you can learn to ride Barney. And you'll be able to meet Maxi at last!

Fiona

| Subject: | Great news! | Date: | April 23 |

Hi Fiona,

Mom says I can come! She's going to call your mom to make the arrangements.

I can't wait.

Emily

| Subject: | Cool! | Date: | April 24 |

Hi Emily,

I'm counting the days!

Fiona

Chapter 7
A Worrying Time

Subject:	Maxi	Date:	May 5

Hi Emily,

This will have to be a short e-mail. We're taking Maxi to the vet. She's been very tired lately. Mom says she's probably just a bit run down, but I can't help worrying.

Fiona

Subject:	Poor Maxi	Date:	May 5

I hope she's okay. Let me know what the vet says.

Emily

Subject:	Nothing to worry about	Date:	May 5

Hi again,

We're back from the vet. Maxi is fine. We have to give her some vitamins, but there's nothing to worry about!

Fiona

P.S. Only a few more weeks till summer break!

Chapter 8
Summer Vacation at Last!

Summer vacation finally came, and Emily took the train to Murgon. During the trip, she thought about all the things she would do with Fiona and Maxi. She couldn't wait to go for a walk along the beach. She wanted Fiona to take her to the place where she had launched her message in a bottle, all those months ago. "I hope Fiona brings Maxi to the station!" she thought.

Finally, the train arrived in Murgon. Emily gathered up her luggage, and climbed down onto the platform.

Emily saw four people standing together on the platform, and easily recognized Fiona from her photo. The others were obviously Fiona's parents and Stu. But there was no dog with them. "Oh no!" she thought. "I hope Maxi's okay."

She heard a shout. "Emily!" Before she knew it, Fiona was hugging her, and laughing, "You're here! You're finally here!"

After everyone had been introduced, and Emily's bags had been loaded into the car, they set off for Murgon Apple Grove. On the way, Stu said to Emily, "So, did Fiona tell you that she's got a surprise for you at home?"

"No!" said Emily. "What is it?"

Fiona laughed. "You'll have to wait and see!"

When they arrived at the farm, Fiona said, "Come and meet Maxi."

Emily's heart leaped. Maxi was okay after all! She followed Fiona and Stu to a small wooden shed. She opened the door and stepped into the shed.

There, on a blanket in the corner of the shed, lay a beautiful border collie, and five tiny balls of black-and-white fluff.

"Emily," said Fiona softly, "meet Maxi – and her puppies!"

"Why didn't you tell me?" gasped Emily. "I was so worried about Maxi! When I didn't see her at the train station, I thought something terrible had happened!"

"I didn't mean to frighten you," said Fiona. "I just wanted to surprise you! *This* is why Maxi was so tired!"

Emily knelt down beside Maxi and the puppies. "They're so cute!" she whispered as she patted Maxi. "This is a great surprise!"

Stu nudged Fiona. "Go on," he said, "ask her."

Fiona hesitated. "Well," she said to Emily, "I know you said that you weren't ready to have another dog, but ... would you like to have one of Maxi's puppies?"

Emily was speechless.

"Only if you want to," Fiona continued. "My mom has already spoken to your mom about it, and she thinks it's a great idea."

Emily looked at Maxi and the puppies. "Another dog?" she said quietly. She stroked one of the puppies gently.

"I'll always miss Patch," she said at last. "But I would *love* to have one of Maxi's puppies!"

"That's great!" cried Fiona. "They're not old enough to take yet. But you could always come back at the end of the summer to get it – or I could bring it to you!"

"Which one are you going to choose?" Stu asked.

Emily looked at the squirmy, bright-eyed puppies. Gently, she picked up the smallest one, and held it to her cheek. "This one," she said softly. "I'm going to call her *Mini.*"

Epilogue

Subject:	Seeking Emily	Date:	August 15

Dear Emily,

My name is Tony, and I am 12 years old. I live in Fairfield. I found your message in a bottle when I was at the beach.

I don't know anyone named Fiona, so I won't be able to help you find her. Maybe we could be penpals instead?

I was sorry to hear about Patch. I'd love to have a dog, but we live in a very small apartment, and Mom says that there isn't enough room.

It was a good idea to put your e-mail address on the message. E-mails are much faster than bottles!

Please reply soon!

Your new friend,
Tony